Biscuit Blast Off!

'Biscuit Blast Off!'

An original concept by Clare Helen Welsh

© Clare Helen Welsh

Illustrated by Sophia Touliatou

Published by MAVERICK ARTS PUBLISHING LTD

Studio 3A, City Business Centre, 6 Brighton Road,

Horsham, West Sussex, RH13 5BB

© Maverick Arts Publishing Limited May 2017

+44 (0)1403 256941

A CIP catalogue record for this book is available at the British Library.

ISBN 978-1-84886-236-4

www.maverickbooks.co.uk

Purple

This book is rated as: Purple Band (Guided Reading)
The original picture book text for this story has been
modified by the author to be an early reader.

Biscuit Blast Off!

By **Clare Helen Welsh**

Illustrated by **Sophia Touliatou**

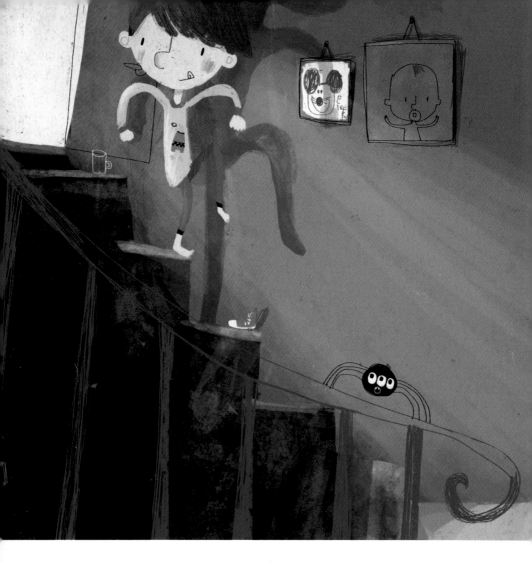

Oliver was a good boy.

Oliver was a kind boy.

Oliver shouldn't have been sneaking into the kitchen

for a midnight snack but he was hungry.

He crept down, down, down the dark, dark stairs.

He reached up, up, up onto the top, top shelf...

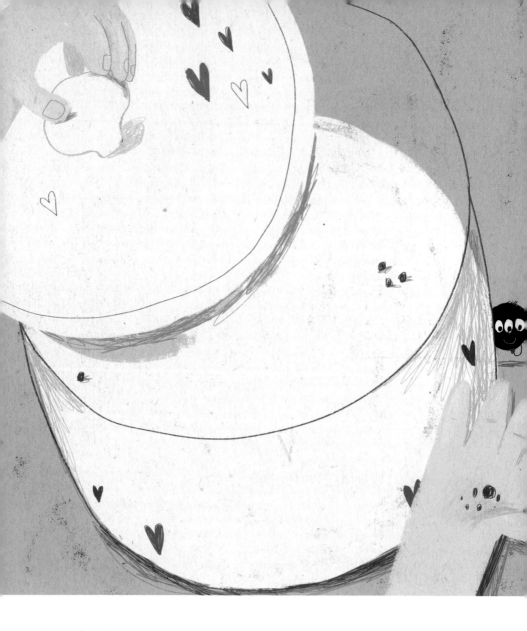

But the biscuit tin was empty!

"Oh no! Where are all the cookies?" said Oliver.

"Where are the flapjacks?"

Just then, Oliver heard a sound in the dark kitchen.

Was it a giant? Or perhaps a burglar? Or even a

troll? Or mice?

MICE!

A gang of sneaky pirate mice were stealing Oliver's biscuits! Where were they going?

The mice went out to the garden.

Their leader was called Captain McSqueaky.

"Aharr, me squeakies!" he yelled. "Great work!"

But the pirate mice were not eating the biscuits.

The pirate mice were making...

Rockets!

They were building biscuit rockets to

fly to the moon!

12

Captain McSqueaky shouted,

"Climb aboard! Let's find some cheese!"

But the flapjacks were too heavy.

The wafers were too light.

The shortbread was too crumbly and the

nutty biscuits were too lumpy and bumpy.

Just when the pirate mice were about

to give up...

"I'll build you a rocket!" Oliver said.

Oliver and the mice got busy.

It took a long, long time, but at last ...

...The Jolly Dodger was ready for take-off!

"We're off to the moon," said Oliver.

"Five... four... three... two... one... BLAST OFF!"

They whooshed up into the dark, dark sky

and landed on the round, cheesy moon.

The mice started to dig. They dug and dug

and dug until... Grrrrrrr!

Their tummies couldn't wait another second!

WAIT! Where is Captain McSqueaky?

Hiccup! Captain McSqueaky

was eating the biscuit rocket!

"How are we going to get home?"

cried the mice.

"You're pirates!" said Oliver,

"What you need is a..."

"A pirate ship to steer you to earth!

We can make it from cheese!"

Soon the ship was ready.

BRIE O' BOOTY

"Let's go home," said Oliver.

They floated down, down, down into

the dark, dark sky until...

"Land ahoy!"

They landed safely in Oliver's garden.

"Phew!"

Oliver was a good boy.

Oliver was a kind boy.

Oliver shouldn't have been sneaking about

in the middle of the night, but he was sleepy.

And so were the mice.

Quiz

1. Why is Oliver sneaking in the kitchen?

a) Because he was a good boy

b) Because he was hungry

c) Because he was a kind boy

2. What kind of mice steal the biscuits?

a) Space mice

b) Pirate mice

c) Cowboy mice

3. Why do the mice steal biscuits?

a) To eat

b) To save for another day

c) To build rockets

4. Why can't Oliver and the mice use the biscuit rocket to go home?

a) It breaks down

b) McSqueaky eats it

c) It is too heavy

5. What is the name of the first rocket?

a) The Jolly Dodger

b) The Brie Pearl

c) The Flying Crunchman

Turn over for answers

Book Bands for Guided Reading

The Institute of Education book banding system is a scale of colours that reflects the various levels of reading difficulty. The bands are assigned by taking into account the content, the language style, the layout and phonics.

Maverick Early Readers are a bright, attractive range of books covering the pink to purple bands. All of these books have been book banded for guided reading to the industry standard and edited by a leading educational consultant.

Pink

Red

Yellow

Blue

Green

Orange

Turquoise

Purple

Gold

White

To view the whole Maverick Readers scheme, visit our website at
www.maverickearlyreaders.com

Or scan the QR code above to view our scheme instantly!

Quiz Answers: 1b, 2b, 3c, 4b, 5a